This Facebook Workbook and Planner Belongs to:

If found, contact me here:

Phone: ____________________________
Email: ____________________________
Address ____________________________

Dedicated To

YOU and my clients

Published by
GreyChild Communications
Toronto, ON

Facebook Workbook and Planner / Dwainia Grey
ISBN-13: 978-0994888846

ISBN-10: 0994888848

WHAT IS THIS?

This is the **Facebook Workbook and Planner** that will help you succeed with Facebook for your Empowerpreneur business. The book is based on the training in Awesome Nation Engagement; it's a companion book as well as a standalone workbook and planner. The Workbook Section of the book helps you create a Facebook strategy for the year and clarify your Facebook goals and tactics (action steps). The Planner Section of the book helps you plan your monthly Facebook strategy and track your monthly actions and milestones to get a clear picture of your Facebook Return on Investment (ROI).

By having a plan you leverage your time, reach targets (people and goals), add automation and measure success.

HOW TO USE THIS WORKBOOK

The first part is the Strategy Workbook which includes worksheets and checklists for you to complete. This helps you develop the Facebook Marketing Plan and success strategy for the coming months.

1. Objective
2. Audience
3. Style Guide
4. Engagement in 15 Minutes
5. Do's & Don'ts
6. Planning
7. Facebook Post Ideas
8. 52 Weeks
9. Facebook Profile Worksheet
10. Facebook Page Worksheet
11. Facebook Group Worksheet
12. Getting Started Cheat Sheet
13. Blog Stats
14. Facebook Yearly Stats

The second section is the **Facebook Action Planner**:

1. Monthly Calendar
2. Monthly Success Tracker
3. Monthly Stats
4. Status Updates
5. Facebook Ad Planner
6. Facebook Campaign Planner
7. To Do
8. Notes

The planner section helps you plan your Facebook posts and engagement for the next 12 months. Each month includes monthly planning tools as well as metrics trackers. At the end of each month review the month and start planning for the new month. It's very important to complete your success tracker as it helps you to duplicate success.

The downloadable PDF contains 40 pages and allows you to print pages as needed.

FACEBOOK TODAY

What is the biggest challenge that you are facing right now with Facebook?

What do you hope to accomplish?

What have you done so far to get your Facebook campaign started?

How much time do you currently spend on Facebook a week?

Are you directing Facebook fans to your email list?

Are you currently using any of the following tools?

- ☐ Facebook
- ☐ Linkedin
- ☐ Twitter
- ☐ YouTube
- ☐ Pinterest
- ☐ Google+
- ☐ Instagram
- ☐ Other sites

facebook MARKETING

WORKBOOK

Objective

facebook
MARKETING

Objective Overall Facebook objective for the year.

- Increase reach
- Build your brand
- Engage influencers and connectors
- Increase customer loyalty
- Drive people to events
- Improve customer service
- Generate leads and sales
- Convert leads to sales

Short-term

Goal # 1 –

Deadline

Action Plan

Goal Met ☐ Yes ☐NO

Goal # 2 –

Deadline

Action Plan

Goal Met ☐ Yes ☐NO

Goal # 3 –

Deadline

Action Plan

Goal Met ☐ Yes ☐NO

Long-term

Goal –

Deadline

Action Plan

Goal Met ☐ Yes ☐NO

Monthly Goal Setter

Set realistic achievable goals for each month.
Goals can be a number of posts or number of new followers to engagement. Make sure it's measurable.

January	February
Goal Met ☐ Yes ☐NO	Goal Met ☐ Yes ☐NO
March	April
Goal Met ☐ Yes ☐NO	Goal Met ☐ Yes ☐NO
May	June
Goal Met ☐ Yes ☐NO	Goal Met ☐ Yes ☐NO
July	August
Goal Met ☐ Yes ☐NO	Goal Met ☐ Yes ☐NO
September	October
Goal Met ☐ Yes ☐NO	Goal Met ☐ Yes ☐NO
November	December
Goal Met ☐ Yes ☐NO	Goal Met ☐ Yes ☐NO

Audience

Your Audience

- ☐ Existing clients
- ☐ Prospective clients

Where they are hanging out:

- ☐ Facebook
- ☐ Twitter
- ☐ Pinterest
- ☐ Instagram
- ☐ Google+
- ☐
- ☐
- ☐

Who Are Your Competitors? – How Do They Use Facebook? – How Are You Different?

What Keeps Your Client up at Night?

How Does Your Product / Service Solve the Problem?

List 3 Successes You Have Had with Clients

Think RESULTS

Audience

What Words or Phrases Do Your Clients Use To Describe the Problem	What Words or Phrases Do Your Clients Use When They Are Looking for the Solution? (KEYWORDS)

Your Avatar

Name (fictitious)

Gender:

Age:

Profession:

Marital & Family Status:

Associations:

Location (city, neighborhood, or postal code):

Style Guide

facebook MARKETING

Image Text 1

Font
Size
Style
Color
Hex
RGB
CMYK

Image Text 2

Font
Size
Style
Color
Hex
RGB
CMYK

Watermark Text 1

Font
Size
Style
Color
Hex
RGB
CMYK

Image Sizes

Profile 180 x 180 px
Tab 111 x 74 px
Group 801 x 250
Event 785 x 295

Cover Image Template 851 x 315 px

Use your cover image for promotions and campaigns.

Post Template 540 x any length px

Show placement of graphics, watermark, text alignment, borders etc.

Notes

Separate post templates for blog posts, quotes, promotions, etc?

Create templates using Photoshop, Fireworks, Canva or Picmonkey.

Voice, tone, hashtags, abbreviations, spellings and punctuation to use:

15 Minutes A Day of Engagement

	Day 1	Day 2
3-5 Minutes	**Share, like, comment on other people's content.**	**Share, like, and comment on other people's content.**
1-5 Minutes	**Notifications** ☐ Answer Comments (Good and Bad) ☐ Respond to Messages ☐ Comment &/or like posts your tagged in	**Notifications** ☐ Answer Comments (Good and Bad) ☐ Respond to Messages
1-5 Minutes	**Group Interaction** Participate in groups by posting content, answering questions and starting the conversation	**Make A New Friend** ☐ Influencers ☐ Current, Past and Future Clients ☐ Future Collaborators ☐ Family and Friends ☐ Approve Friend Request

WHEN THE MOOD STRIKES UPDATE YOUR STATUS

Increase Engagement by Integrating Facebook on Your Website

- ☐ Facebook Profile buttons
- ☐ Facebook Widget
- ☐ Facebook Share buttons
- ☐ Embed Facebook posts on blog posts

Schedule

- ☐ Schedule other peoples' posts using scheduling tools
- ☐ Schedule your blog posts
- ☐ Day published
- ☐ 1 week later
- ☐ 1 month later

Facebook Do's and Don'ts

facebook MARKETING

- ☐ Always follow the rules and regulations for Facebook. If you don't you can get your account suspended. Read the Facebook Page Terms.
- ☐ Do commit the time and effort to maintain your Facebook marketing plan.
- ☐ Do pay attention to social media ethics
- ☐ Do answer all messages / comments in a timely manner.
- ☐ Do create a social media marketing plan, but adjust your specific tactics as you go. Be flexible and take the time to find out what works and what doesn't work.
- ☐ Do go local with Facebook, it's a great opportunity to take online relationships offline.
- ☐ Do listen to your clients through your social media and respond where appropriate
- ☐ Do participate. Join the conversation by commenting and participating in groups.
- ☐ Do pay attention to the metrics and analytics of your campaign.
- ☐ Do prepare to deal with how online users change, alter or use your brand's message. Have a plan for both good and bad customer feedback.
- ☐ Do support the promotional campaigns of other non-competitive businesses and your fans.
- ☐ Remember short posts are better. Add a short description to links and include images and video.
- ☐ Do tag people and companies where appropriate
- ☐ Don't forget to add attribution when it's not your content.
- ☐ Don't just post your own content
- ☐ Don't post photos that will embarrass or humiliate someone or that are unflattering
- ☐ Don't share every moment of your day
- ☐ Don't be disrespectful, offensive, vulgar or use language considered to be inflammatory. Don't be rude or difficult to deal with when engaging with your fans
- ☐ Don't delete comments unless it's spam. Learn how to deal with negative feedback.
- ☐ Don't lie to your audience or hide the fact that you are advertising to them. Always be transparent with your intentions
- ☐ Don't over post on Facebook. Posting 1-2 times a day depending on your audience is good. If you are posting more than 2 times a day ensure it adds value.
- ☐ Don't overdo it when promoting your business. You want to use social media to build relationships not overwhelm people with ads.
- ☐ Don't have vague posts. Using one word posts that don't mean anything are not helpful.
- ☐ Don't spam!

Notes

Day-to-Day Management

How many times a week will you post on Facebook?
Suggested number of times a week to post :2x daily

What days and times will you post?

How far ahead do you want to plan content?

How often will you promote your own content (blog posts, events, products and services) versus other peoples content?

What type of content are you going to share? Review the Post Idea Sheet. What you share needs to bring value - always think "What's in it for me?" Try for a combination of educating, and engaging. You are aiming to get them interested in you, your brand, and your business.

Who will create content? Images / Video / Copy

Who will post content?

Who will manage your Facebook campaigns?

Who will track, monitor, and report?

Planning

Do you want to assign posts to certain days a week? Throwback Thursday, Follow Friday, or make up your own

	Themed Post	Create Content	Publish Content
Monday			
Tuesday			
Wednesday			
Thursday			
Friday			
Saturday			
Sunday			

Resources

- ☐ Experienced Writer
- ☐ Professional Photos / Photo shoot
- ☐ Professional Videos / Video shoot
- ☐ Branded Graphics

Facebook Policy

Develop your Facebook Policy.
Read the Do's and Don'ts of Facebook. What are the policy's you will have for you Empowerpreneur business?

- Rules of engagement
- How to handle customer service
- What to say and what not to say
- Workflow / Schedule
- How to handle negative feedback /criticism
  - Clients, media or competitors

Budget

Startup and launch budget
Campaign budgets
Ongoing management budget
- Advertising
- Design
- Tools (Canva, Pic Monkey, Hootsuite, Buffer, etc)

Metrics

On a weekly and/or monthly basis review your online metrics. Use Google Analytics in conjunction with bitly, and the Facebook Insights to track and monitor your success. Also use Buffer and Hootsuite reporting tools.

Learn more about your return on investment (ROI – time and money) as well as which posts brings the most traffic, engagement and conversion.

Take time to complete the Blog Stats, Monthly Success Tracker and The Monthly And Yearly Social Media Stats.

Va Va VooM ™

Va Va VooM ™ (Content Marketing Ratio)

Value – 60% - Tips, tutorials, and instructional useful and helpful posts

List 3 topics that you can post that will add value

Visual – 20% - Make use of images and videos

List 3 ways you can use images / videos in social media

Voice – 10% - Show your personality – personal posts about you, showing your life, and a behind the scenes

List 3 posts that will show your personality

Marketing – 10% - Promotional posts to sell and promote your products and services

List 3 products / services you want to sell / promote via social media

Content Ideas for Facebook

1	**Valuable & Useful Information**	2	**Blog Posts** Ensure every blog has a branded image	3	**Influencers Posts**	4	**Personal Posts**
5	**Opinions Matter** Ask your Facebook Fans opinions on products, services, packaging, new product ideas, promotions, processes etc.	6	**Spotlight a Fan** Choose one fan per week (or month) to spotlight on your page.	7	**Tips and Tricks** Post tips and tricks as memes or lists.	8	**Events, Workshops & Seminars** Share online and offline events you are hosting or attending
9	**Like Posts** Post something fun on your page and ask people to "like" it. Example: "Like this" if you agree	10	**Emotional / funny posts** Memes, jokes and gifs are very popular.	11	**Fill in the Blanks** Create some fun conversation around a fill-in-the-blank. Example: Fill-in-the-blank: The first thing I do in the morning is…	12	**Business News** Updates about your business and industry.
13	**Quotes** Post quotes that will motivate + inspire your audience.	14	**Products / Services** Create albums around products and services. Announce new products and services.	15	**Video / Photos** Pictures of you and your products and don't forget people love to watch videos	16	**Questions / Poll** Ask community what they think
17	**Promotions** Promote your products, services, sales and coupons. Use contests, giveaways and sweepstakes	18	**Live Events** Live Q & A Live Video	19	**Sales** Use Facebook offers for the hard sell; use free resources and tools for the soft sell.	20	**Celebrate Milestones / Anniversaries** Almost at 1,000 fans? Offer a prize when you reach a numbered milestone.

Plan out 52 weeks of Tips, Quotes, etc
52 Weeks of ___________________________

1		27	
2		28	
3		29	
4		30	
5		31	
6		32	
7		33	
8		34	
9		35	
10		36	
11		37	
12		38	
13		39	
14		40	
15		41	
16		42	
17		43	
18		44	
19		45	
20		46	
21		47	
22		48	
23		49	
24		50	
25		51	
26		52	

Facebook Profile

facebook
MARKETING

Name:

Places You Lived: Current, Hometown, Other

Contact and Basic Info

Phone Number: sync with your mobile include your business number under work

Address: Business Address

Other Accounts: Add all your social media profiles

Website:

Email: List your generic business email along with your personal (see privacy settings) so that friends can find you

Birth Date:

Optional – Who You're Interested In, Languages, Religious, Political party

Family and Relationships

Marital and Family Status:

Family Members:

Work and Education

Be sure to link your current work with your company page.

What Colleges and High Schools did you attend?

Personal use. Interaction with friends and family. Limited to 5,000 friends. Promotional post not allowed.

Facebook Profile

facebook MARKETING

About You

Other Names:

Favorite Quotes:

Life Events

Work and Education

Family and Relationships

Home and Living

Health and Wellness

Travel and Experience

Personal use. Interaction with friends and family. Limited to 5,000 friends. Promotional post not allowed.

Facebook Page

facebook MARKETING

Objective

Name
Your Business Name, Service or Product Name, Your Name (70 characters)

Consider your Facebook Address:

Purpose of Page
"What's in it For Me?"

Products and Services Promoted

Category

Only choose local business if you have a physical location.

- Enables Facebook checki-ns.
- Shows address instead of short description.
- Can be changed at a later date.

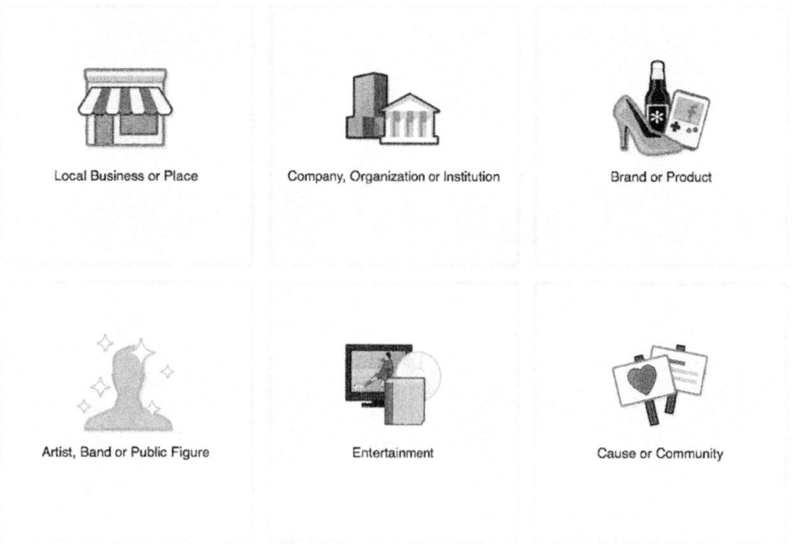

Facebook Page

facebook MARKETING

Profile Image
180 x 180 px
Logo or Professional Image

Cover Image
851 x 315 px
Cannot have more than 20% text – Can now include call to action

About Short Description (155 characters)

Website URL:

About Long Description (30k+ characters)

Facebook Page

facebook MARKETING

Tabs / Apps

Sort Default: About, Photo, Likes, Videos
Optional: Events, Notes
Recommended: Other Social Media, Blog, Etsy, Shopify

Call To Action

Book Now, Call Now, Contact Us, Send Money, Use App, Play Game, Shop Now, Sign Up, Watch Video

Contact Info

- ☐ Phone
- ☐ Website
- ☐ Email
- ☐ Address (Will be used for check-in)

Settings

- ☐ General
- ☐ Message
- ☐ Page Info
- ☐ Post Attributes
- ☐ Notifications
- ☐ Page Roles
- ☐ People and Other Pages
- ☐ Apps

Milestones

Facebook Group

facebook MARKETING

Objective	Name Your Business Name, Service or Product Name, Catchy Name or Name of Your Awesome Nation
Purpose of Group "What's in it For Me?"	Support Offered

Products and Services Promoted

Facebook Group

facebook MARKETING

Privacy

☐ Public – Everyone can see everything (Best for community service)

☐ Secret – No one can see posts, or members. Group is not searchable. (Best for training)

☐ Closed – Public can not see posts but can see members, group shows up in search and recommendations. (Best to build Awesome Nation – shows exclusivity)

Promote Your Facebook Group

☐ Invite friends and fans

☐ Invite mailing list

	Use **Daily Theme** for conversation starters and consistency Make it fun and motivational. Try to add A Promo Day
Monday	
Tuesday	
Wednesday	
Thursday	
Friday	
Saturday	
Sunday	

Manage the Group

☐ Welcome new members individually by using the @ tag. Allows members to say hello and introduce themselves.

☐ Be natural – You may not agree with all posts , but every post is not for you. People join groups looking for support and affinity. Allow the group to progress, expand and evolve without interference.

☐ Set clear guidelines and rules

☐ Moderate group

☐ Start the conversation outside of daily themes: Ask Questions, Create Polls, Make Observations

☐ Invite Group to Events - Offline, Online such as Webinars etc

☐ Host Group Challenges - 7 Day, 10 Day, 21 Day, 30 Day – Each day post a new challenge to the group.

Facebook Group

Guidelines

Use your about section (2000 characters) to post guidelines for the group.

- ☐ Group purpose
- ☐ Daily themes
- ☐ What to expect
- ☐ Stance on promotions
- ☐ Stance on spam – what is considered spam
- ☐ Include Opt-in offer
- ☐ Include link to guidelines listed on your website for better viewing on mobile device.

Moderate Group

- ☐ Know what you will and will not allow.
- ☐ Allow members to post.
- ☐ Watch for trolls, spammers and losers.
- ☐ Stick to your rules in the guidelines
- ☐ Don't be afraid to remove posts
- ☐ Don't be afraid to remove and block people
- ☐ Be prepared to update guidelines
- ☐ Allow the group to self-moderate – members will ignore or complain when necessary or it may start a lively discussion
- ☐ Create hard and fast rules: Promotion, Hurtful, Threatening, Slandering

Group Guidelines

Don't Be First

- ☐ Being on Facebook all the time is not efficient and leaves an impression
- ☐ People start expecting you to answer first
- ☐ People will expect free coaching
- ☐ Deters people from participating

Ask for The Sale

- ☐ Announce your products and services
- ☐ Use Call to Action in post
- ☐ Pre announce – REMEMBER EXCLUSIVITY
- ☐ Don't over advertise or only post from your blog

Notes

Getting Started Cheat Sheet

facebook MARKETING

Branding

- ☐ I have a clear description of who my target audience is.
- ☐ My preferred client is using Facebook
- ☐ I have included a professional photo on my personal profile?
- ☐ My Facebook Page name is easy to find, follow, and connect with.
    - ☐ It's my business name, brand name or based on an SEO keyword.
    - ☐ It's the same as my other social media profile names for consistency
- ☐ I have a completed Facebook Page with a logo, and branded cover?
- ☐ About section includes keywords and website URL - reflects my voice and brand
- ☐ I have claimed my custom Facebook URL
- ☐ I know what personality/ brand message and image I want to communicate.
- ☐ I have included a professional email address - @yourwebsite.com
- ☐ I have included my business location (where applicable - at least put country)
- ☐ I ensure I use the correct NAP (Name, Address and Phone number - where applicable)
- ☐ I link to other social media profiles (where applicable)

Planning

- ☐ I know my Facebook objective
- ☐ I have defined my Facebook marketing goals and know how I will track them.
- ☐ I've created systems to test and track my social media marketing goals and tactics.
- ☐ I have a *Social Media Marketing Plan* that I use to help guide my online marketing and I've integrated my Facebook marketing tactics into my overall social media marketing strategies.
- ☐ I've use relevant dashboards and automation tools to optimize my time such as Hootsuite.
- ☐ I've documented the systems and tools I use, so it can be easily delegated.
- ☐ I use insights to create targeted posts and know the best day and time for engagement
- ☐ I create super targeted ads with Facebook Advertising
- ☐ I have a (monthly/ weekly / daily) posting schedule for Facebook
- ☐ I have a (monthly/ weekly/ daily) Facebook engagement schedule
    - ☐ Post status updates and in groups
    - ☐ Respond to all messages and comments on your page
    - ☐ Tag people when you post their content
    - ☐ Comment as your page
- ☐ I have a strategy to capture leads from Facebook and to get fans to buy

Getting Started Cheat Sheet

facebook MARKETING

Content

- ☐ I have developed a system to find valuable content to share on Facebook
- ☐ I make sure I share a good mix of content (*Va Va VooM* – Value, Voice, Visual and Marketing)
- ☐ I use a Call To Action in posts
- ☐ I'm creating specific promotions and offers for my Facebook audience - *EXCLUSIVE*.
- ☐ I periodically change my Facebook cover photo to highlight my products / services, product launches and promotions
- ☐ I use an editorial calendar to layout content for my blog, and Facebook posts.
- ☐ I schedule blog posts as they are published, a week later, and a month later.
- ☐ I create a schedule to promote old blog posts.
- ☐ I use Facebook Insights to find the optimal day and time to post content for maximum engagement
- ☐ I follow the top blogs in my industry to stay on top of trends.
- ☐ I create specific content to share on Facebook
- ☐ I always check for grammar and spelling

Facebook Tools

- ☐ Facebook Insights
- ☐ Woobox
- ☐ Hootsuite
- ☐ Buffer
- ☐ Canva
- ☐ Picmonkey
- ☐ Pixlr

Yearly Stats

Year	Total Fans		# of Shares		# of Posts		# of Likes		# of Comments		# of Clicks to Website	
	Goal	Actual	Goal	Actual	Goal	Actual	Goal	Actual	Goal	Actual	Goal	Actual
January												
February												
March												
April												
May												
June												
July												
August												
September												
October												
November												
December												
Yearly Total												

Blog Stats

	Date	Facebook	Twitter	Google+	Pinterest	Instagram	Blog Visits
1							
2							
3							
4							
5							
6							
7							
8							
9							
10							
11							
12							
13							
14							
15							
16							
17							
18							
19							
20							
21							
22							
23							
24							
25							
26							
27							
28							
29							
30							
31							
32							
33							
34							
35							
36							
37							
38							
39							
40							
41							
42							
43							
44							
45							
46							
47							
48							
49							
50							
51							
52							

facebook MARKETING

PLANNER

Editorial Calendar

Month

SUNDAY	MONDAY	TUESDAY	WEDNESDAY	THURSDAY	FRIDAY	SATURDAY

Notes

Acknowledge and Celebrate Your Success

Month:

Total Likes

Post with most engagement (shares, likes, comments) on Facebook

---

Post with most clicks

Blog post with most traffic from Facebook

This month I learned

A record I broke this month

My celebration this month

Next month I plan to do the same

Next month I plan to try (new)

Monthly Stats

GOAL:

Total Fans	New Fans	# of Posts	# of Shares	# of Likes	# of Comments	Reach	# of Clicks	# of Clicks to Website

EMAIL SUBSCRIBERS FROM FACEBOOK	
ENGAGEMENT	
Post with most shares	
Post with most likes	
Post with most comments	
Post with most clicks	

BOOSTS

Spend $	# of Shares	# of Likes	# of Comments	Reach	# of Clicks

FACEBOOK ADS

Spend $		Results	

Status Updates

facebook MARKETING

Facebook Status Updates	Date	Time	✓

Campaign Manager

facebook MARKETING

Product / Service Campaign

Campaign	
Description	
Product / Service Newsletter Contest / Giveaway	
Start	End
Objective	
Target Audience	
Budget$ / Cost$ / Return$	
Landing Page	
Tracking Link	
Days and Time	
Winner / Date Notified	

Image

- ☐ Blog Post Announcement
- ☐ Blog Post Follow-up
- ☐ Autoresponder Setup
- ☐ Ad Campaign
  - Budget$
  - Cost$
  - Return$
  - Click Thru Rate
  - CPC (Cost per Click)
- ☐ Conversion Rate
- ☐ Hashtag
- ☐ Coupon Code (if applicable)

Advertising Campaign

Campaign	
Boost / Ad	
Description	
Start	End
Objective	
Target Audience	
Budget$ / Cost Per Day$	
Landing Page	
Tracking Link	

Text

Demographic

Image

Ad Planner

facebook MARKETING

Campaign ______________________

Title / Headline (25 Characters) ______________________

Description (90 Characters) ______________________

Detailed Text (200 Characters only seen on desktop) ______________________

Call to Action ______________________

Start & End Date ______________________

Objective ______________________

Target Audience ______________________

Button ______________________

Budget$ / Cost$ / Return$ ______________________

Landing Page ______________________

Tracking Link ______________________

Reach ______________________

Leads Generated ______________________

Cost Per Lead ______________________

Ad Planner

facebook MARKETING

Image

- ☐ Image
- ☐ Ad Copy
- ☐ Ad Distribution (Desktop or Newsfeed)
- ☐ Audience (Demographics + Interests)
- ☐ Ad Campaign
  - Budget$
  - Cost$
  - Return$
  - Click Thru Rate
  - CPC (Cost per Click)
- ☐ Conversion Rate

To Do

	Priority	Completed

Month

SUNDAY	MONDAY	TUESDAY	WEDNESDAY	THURSDAY	FRIDAY	SATURDAY

Notes

Acknowledge and Celebrate Your Success

Month:

Total Likes

Post with most engagement (shares, likes, comments) on Facebook

---

Post with most clicks

Blog post with most traffic from Facebook

This month I learned

A record I broke this month

My celebration this month

Next month I plan to do the same

Next month I plan to try (new)

Monthly Stats

GOAL:

Total Fans	New Fans	# of Posts	# of Shares	# of Likes	# of Comments	Reach	# of Clicks	# of Clicks to Website

EMAIL SUBSCRIBERS FROM FACEBOOK	

ENGAGEMENT

Post with most shares	
Post with most likes	
Post with most comments	
Post with most clicks	

BOOSTS

Spend $	# of Shares	# of Likes	# of Comments	Reach	# of Clicks

FACEBOOK ADS

Spend $		Results	

Status Updates

Facebook Status Updates	Date	Time	✓

Campaign Manager

facebook MARKETING

Product / Service Campaign

Campaign	
Description	
Product / Service Newsletter Contest / Giveaway	
Start	End
Objective	
Target Audience	
Budget$ / Cost$ / Return$	
Landing Page	
Tracking Link	
Days and Time	
Winner / Date Notified	

Image

- ☐ Blog Post Announcement
- ☐ Blog Post Follow-up
- ☐ Autoresponder Setup
- ☐ Ad Campaign
  - Budget$
  - Cost$
  - Return$
  - Click Thru Rate
  - CPC (Cost per Click)
- ☐ Conversion Rate
- ☐ Hashtag
- ☐ Coupon Code (if applicable)

Advertising Campaign

Campaign	
Boost / Ad	
Description	
Start	End
Objective	
Target Audience	
Budget$ / Cost Per Day$	
Landing Page	
Tracking Link	

Text	Demographic

Image

Ad Planner

facebook MARKETING

Campaign ______________________________

Title / Headline (25 Characters) ______________________________

Description (90 Characters) ______________________________

Detailed Text (200 Characters only seen on desktop) ______________________________

Call to Action ______________________________

Start & End Date ______________________________

Objective ______________________________

Target Audience ______________________________

Button ______________________________

Budget$ / Cost$ / Return$ ______________________________

Landing Page ______________________________

Tracking Link ______________________________

Reach ______________________________

Leads Generated ______________________________

Cost Per Lead ______________________________

Image

- ☐ Image
- ☐ Ad Copy
- ☐ Ad Distribution (Desktop or Newsfeed)
- ☐ Audience (Demographics + Interests)
- ☐ Ad Campaign
  - Budget$
  - Cost$
  - Return$
  - Click Thru Rate
  - CPC (Cost per Click)
- ☐ Conversion Rate

To Do

	Priority	Completed

Editorial Calendar

facebook MARKETING

Month

SUNDAY	MONDAY	TUESDAY	WEDNESDAY	THURSDAY	FRIDAY	SATURDAY

Notes

Acknowledge and Celebrate Your Success

Month:

Total Likes

Post with most engagement (shares, likes, comments) on Facebook

---

Post with most clicks

Blog post with most traffic from Facebook

This month I learned

A record I broke this month

My celebration this month

Next month I plan to do the same

Next month I plan to try (new)

Monthly Stats

GOAL:

Total Fans	New Fans	# of Posts	# of Shares	# of Likes	# of Comments	Reach	# of Clicks	# of Clicks to Website

EMAIL SUBSCRIBERS FROM FACEBOOK	
ENGAGEMENT	
Post with most shares	
Post with most likes	
Post with most comments	
Post with most clicks	

BOOSTS

Spend $	# of Shares	# of Likes	# of Comments	Reach	# of Clicks

FACEBOOK ADS

Spend $		Results	

Status Updates

Facebook Status Updates	Date	Time	✓

Campaign Manager

facebook MARKETING

Product / Service Campaign

Campaign	
Description	
Product / Service Newsletter Contest / Giveaway	
Start	End
Objective	
Target Audience	
Budget$ / Cost$ / Return$	
Landing Page	
Tracking Link	
Days and Time	
Winner / Date Notified	

Image

- ☐ Blog Post Announcement
- ☐ Blog Post Follow-up
- ☐ Autoresponder Setup
- ☐ Ad Campaign
  - Budget$
  - Cost$
  - Return$
  - Click Thru Rate
  - CPC (Cost per Click)
- ☐ Conversion Rate
- ☐ Hashtag
- ☐ Coupon Code (if applicable)

Advertising Campaign

Campaign	
Boost / Ad	
Description	
Start	End
Objective	
Target Audience	
Budget$ / Cost Per Day$	
Landing Page	
Tracking Link	

Text	Demographic
	Image

Ad Planner

facebook MARKETING

Campaign ____________________

Title / Headline (25 Characters) ____________________

Description (90 Characters) ____________________

Detailed Text (200 Characters only seen on desktop) ____________________

Call to Action ____________________

Start & End Date ____________________

Objective ____________________

Target Audience ____________________

Button ____________________

Budget$ / Cost$ / Return$ ____________________

Landing Page ____________________

Tracking Link ____________________

Reach ____________________

Leads Generated ____________________

Cost Per Lead ____________________

Ad Planner

facebook MARKETING

Image

- ☐ Image
- ☐ Ad Copy
- ☐ Ad Distribution (Desktop or Newsfeed)
- ☐ Audience (Demographics + Interests)
- ☐ Ad Campaign
  - Budget$
  - Cost$
  - Return$
  - Click Thru Rate
  - CPC (Cost per Click)
- ☐ Conversion Rate

To Do

	Priority	Completed

Editorial Calendar

facebook MARKETING

Month

SUNDAY	MONDAY	TUESDAY	WEDNESDAY	THURSDAY	FRIDAY	SATURDAY

Notes

Success Tracker

facebook MARKETING

Acknowledge and Celebrate Your Success

Month:

Total Likes

Post with most engagement (shares, likes, comments) on Facebook

---

Post with most clicks

Blog post with most traffic from Facebook

This month I learned

A record I broke this month

My celebration this month

Next month I plan to do the same

Next month I plan to try (new)

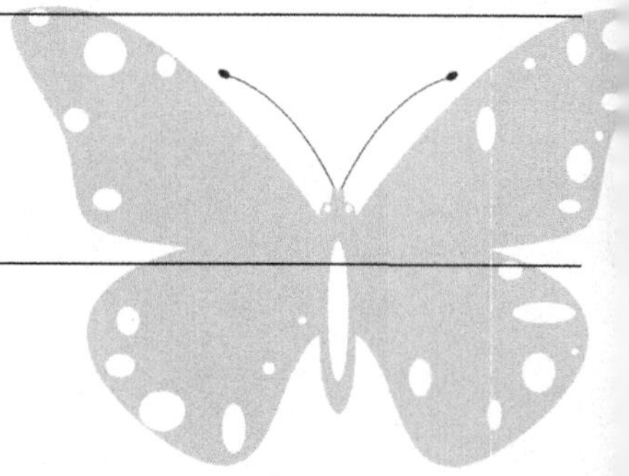

Monthly Stats

GOAL:

Total Fans	New Fans	# of Posts	# of Shares	# of Likes	# of Comments	Reach	# of Clicks	# of Clicks to Website

EMAIL SUBSCRIBERS FROM FACEBOOK	
ENGAGEMENT	
Post with most shares	
Post with most likes	
Post with most comments	
Post with most clicks	

BOOSTS

Spend $	# of Shares	# of Likes	# of Comments	Reach	# of Clicks

FACEBOOK ADS

Spend $		Results	

Status Updates

Facebook Status Updates	Date	Time	✓

Campaign Manager

facebook MARKETING

Product / Service Campaign

Campaign	
Description	
Product / Service Newsletter Contest / Giveaway	
Start	End
Objective	
Target Audience	
Budget$ / Cost$ / Return$	
Landing Page	
Tracking Link	
Days and Time	
Winner / Date Notified	

Image

- ☐ Blog Post Announcement
- ☐ Blog Post Follow-up
- ☐ Autoresponder Setup
- ☐ Ad Campaign
  - Budget$
  - Cost$
  - Return$
  - Click Thru Rate
  - CPC (Cost per Click)
- ☐ Conversion Rate
- ☐ Hashtag
- ☐ Coupon Code (if applicable)

Advertising Campaign

Campaign	
Boost / Ad	
Description	
Start	End
Objective	
Target Audience	
Budget$ / Cost Per Day$	
Landing Page	
Tracking Link	

Text	Demographic
	Image

Ad Planner

facebook
MARKETING

Campaign ______________________

Title / Headline (25 Characters) ______________________

Description (90 Characters) ______________________

Detailed Text (200 Characters only seen on desktop) ______________________

Call to Action ______________________

Start & End Date ______________________

Objective ______________________

Target Audience ______________________

Button ______________________

Budget$ / Cost$ / Return$ ______________________

Landing Page ______________________

Tracking Link ______________________

Reach ______________________

Leads Generated ______________________

Cost Per Lead ______________________

Ad Planner

facebook MARKETING

Image

- ☐ Image
- ☐ Ad Copy
- ☐ Ad Distribution (Desktop or Newsfeed)
- ☐ Audience (Demographics + Interests)
- ☐ Ad Campaign
  - Budget$
  - Cost$
  - Return$
  - Click Thru Rate
  - CPC (Cost per Click)
- ☐ Conversion Rate

To Do

facebook MARKETING

	Priority	Completed

Editorial Calendar

facebook MARKETING

Month

SUNDAY	MONDAY	TUESDAY	WEDNESDAY	THURSDAY	FRIDAY	SATURDAY

Notes

Acknowledge and Celebrate Your Success

Month:

Total Likes

Post with most engagement (shares, likes, comments) on Facebook

---

Post with most clicks

Blog post with most traffic from Facebook

This month I learned

A record I broke this month

My celebration this month

Next month I plan to do the same

Next month I plan to try (new)

Monthly Stats

facebook MARKETING

GOAL:

Total Fans	New Fans	# of Posts	# of Shares	# of Likes	# of Comments	Reach	# of Clicks	# of Clicks to Website

EMAIL SUBSCRIBERS FROM FACEBOOK	
ENGAGEMENT	
Post with most shares	
Post with most likes	
Post with most comments	
Post with most clicks	

BOOSTS

Spend $	# of Shares	# of Likes	# of Comments	Reach	# of Clicks

FACEBOOK ADS

Spend $		Results	

Status Updates

Facebook Status Updates	Date	Time	✓

Campaign Manager

facebook MARKETING

Product / Service Campaign

Campaign	
Description	
Product / Service Newsletter Contest / Giveaway	
Start	End
Objective	
Target Audience	
Budget$ / Cost$ / Return$	
Landing Page	
Tracking Link	
Days and Time	
Winner / Date Notified	

Image

- ☐ Blog Post Announcement
- ☐ Blog Post Follow-up
- ☐ Autoresponder Setup
- ☐ Ad Campaign
  - Budget$
  - Cost$
  - Return$
  - Click Thru Rate
  - CPC (Cost per Click)
- ☐ Conversion Rate
- ☐ Hashtag
- ☐ Coupon Code (if applicable)

Advertising Campaign

Campaign	
Boost / Ad	
Description	
Start	End
Objective	
Target Audience	
Budget$ / Cost Per Day$	
Landing Page	
Tracking Link	

Text

Demographic

Image

Ad Planner

facebook MARKETING

Campaign ______________________________

Title / Headline (25 Characters) ______________________________

Description (90 Characters) ______________________________

Detailed Text (200 Characters only seen on desktop) ______________________________

Call to Action ______________________________

Start & End Date ______________________________

Objective ______________________________

Target Audience ______________________________

Button ______________________________

Budget$ / Cost$ / Return$ ______________________________

Landing Page ______________________________

Tracking Link ______________________________

Reach ______________________________

Leads Generated ______________________________

Cost Per Lead ______________________________

Ad Planner

facebook MARKETING

Image

- [ ] Image
- [ ] Ad Copy
- [ ] Ad Distribution (Desktop or Newsfeed)
- [ ] Audience (Demographics + Interests)
- [ ] Ad Campaign
  - Budget$
  - Cost$
  - Return$
  - Click Thru Rate
  - CPC (Cost per Click)
- [ ] Conversion Rate

	Priority	Completed

Editorial Calendar

facebook MARKETING

Month

SUNDAY	MONDAY	TUESDAY	WEDNESDAY	THURSDAY	FRIDAY	SATURDAY

Notes

Acknowledge and Celebrate Your Success

Month:

Total Likes

Post with most engagement (shares, likes, comments) on Facebook

---

Post with most clicks

Blog post with most traffic from Facebook

This month I learned

A record I broke this month

My celebration this month

Next month I plan to do the same

Next month I plan to try (new)

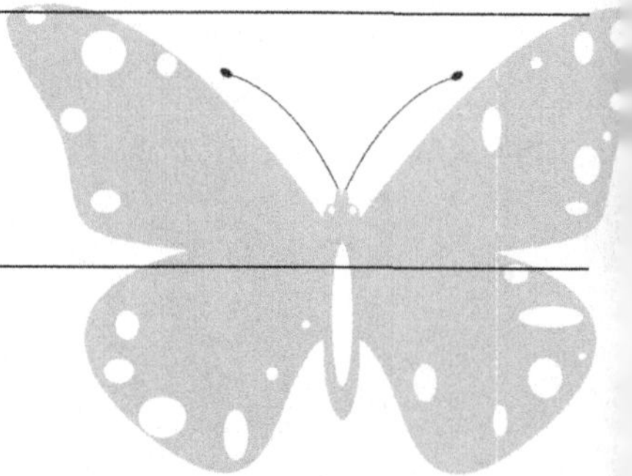

GOAL:

Total Fans	New Fans	# of Posts	# of Shares	# of Likes	# of Comments	Reach	# of Clicks	# of Clicks to Website

EMAIL SUBSCRIBERS FROM FACEBOOK	
ENGAGEMENT	
Post with most shares	
Post with most likes	
Post with most comments	
Post with most clicks	

BOOSTS

Spend $	# of Shares	# of Likes	# of Comments	Reach	# of Clicks

FACEBOOK ADS

Spend $		Results	

Facebook Status Updates	Date	Time	✓

Campaign Manager

facebook MARKETING

Product / Service Campaign

Campaign	
Description	
Product / Service Newsletter Contest / Giveaway	
Start	End
Objective	
Target Audience	
Budget$ / Cost$ / Return$	
Landing Page	
Tracking Link	
Days and Time	
Winner / Date Notified	

Image

- ☐ Blog Post Announcement
- ☐ Blog Post Follow-up
- ☐ Autoresponder Setup
- ☐ Ad Campaign
  - Budget$
  - Cost$
  - Return$
  - Click Thru Rate
  - CPC (Cost per Click)
- ☐ Conversion Rate
- ☐ Hashtag
- ☐ Coupon Code (if applicable)

Advertising Campaign

Campaign	
Boost / Ad	
Description	
Start	End
Objective	
Target Audience	
Budget$ / Cost Per Day$	
Landing Page	
Tracking Link	

Text	Demographic
	Image

Ad Planner

facebook MARKETING

Campaign ______________________

Title / Headline (25 Characters) ______________________

Description (90 Characters) ______________________

Detailed Text (200 Characters only seen on desktop) ______________________

Call to Action ______________________

Start & End Date ______________________

Objective ______________________

Target Audience ______________________

Button ______________________

Budget$ / Cost$ / Return$ ______________________

Landing Page ______________________

Tracking Link ______________________

Reach ______________________

Leads Generated ______________________

Cost Per Lead ______________________

Ad Planner

facebook MARKETING

Image

- ☐ Image
- ☐ Ad Copy
- ☐ Ad Distribution (Desktop or Newsfeed)
- ☐ Audience (Demographics + Interests)
- ☐ Ad Campaign
  - Budget$
  - Cost$
  - Return$
  - Click Thru Rate
  - CPC (Cost per Click)
- ☐ Conversion Rate

To Do

	Priority	Completed

Notes

Editorial Calendar

Month

SUNDAY	MONDAY	TUESDAY	WEDNESDAY	THURSDAY	FRIDAY	SATURDAY

Notes

Acknowledge and Celebrate Your Success

Month:

Total Likes

Post with most engagement (shares, likes, comments) on Facebook

---

Post with most clicks

Blog post with most traffic from Facebook

This month I learned

A record I broke this month

My celebration this month

Next month I plan to do the same

Next month I plan to try (new)

Monthly Stats

GOAL:

Total Fans	New Fans	# of Posts	# of Shares	# of Likes	# of Comments	Reach	# of Clicks	# of Clicks to Website

EMAIL SUBSCRIBERS FROM FACEBOOK	

ENGAGEMENT

Post with most shares	
Post with most likes	
Post with most comments	
Post with most clicks	

BOOSTS

Spend $	# of Shares	# of Likes	# of Comments	Reach	# of Clicks

FACEBOOK ADS

Spend $		Results	

Status Updates

Facebook Status Updates	Date	Time	✓

Campaign Manager

facebook MARKETING

Product / Service Campaign

Campaign	
Description	
Product / Service Newsletter Contest / Giveaway	
Start	End
Objective	
Target Audience	
Budget$ / Cost$ / Return$	
Landing Page	
Tracking Link	
Days and Time	
Winner / Date Notified	

Image

- ☐ Blog Post Announcement
- ☐ Blog Post Follow-up
- ☐ Autoresponder Setup
- ☐ Ad Campaign
  - Budget$
  - Cost$
  - Return$
  - Click Thru Rate
  - CPC (Cost per Click)
- ☐ Conversion Rate
- ☐ Hashtag
- ☐ Coupon Code (if applicable)

Advertising Campaign

Campaign	
Boost / Ad	
Description	
Start	End
Objective	
Target Audience	
Budget$ / Cost Per Day$	
Landing Page	
Tracking Link	

Text	Demographic

	Image

Ad Planner

facebook MARKETING

Campaign ______________________

Title / Headline (25 Characters) ______________________

Description (90 Characters) ______________________

Detailed Text (200 Characters only seen on desktop) ______________________

Call to Action ______________________

Start & End Date ______________________

Objective ______________________

Target Audience ______________________

Button ______________________

Budget$ / Cost$ / Return$ ______________________

Landing Page ______________________

Tracking Link ______________________

Reach ______________________

Leads Generated ______________________

Cost Per Lead ______________________

Ad Planner

facebook MARKETING

Image

- ☐ Image
- ☐ Ad Copy
- ☐ Ad Distribution (Desktop or Newsfeed)
- ☐ Audience (Demographics + Interests)
- ☐ Ad Campaign
  - Budget$
  - Cost$
  - Return$
  - Click Thru Rate
  - CPC (Cost per Click)
- ☐ Conversion Rate

To Do

	Priority	Completed

Editorial Calendar

facebook MARKETING

Month

SUNDAY	MONDAY	TUESDAY	WEDNESDAY	THURSDAY	FRIDAY	SATURDAY

Notes

Acknowledge and Celebrate Your Success

Month:

Total Likes

Post with most engagement (shares, likes, comments) on Facebook

Post with most clicks

Blog post with most traffic from Facebook

This month I learned

A record I broke this month

My celebration this month

Next month I plan to do the same

Next month I plan to try (new)

Monthly Stats

GOAL:

Total Fans	New Fans	# of Posts	# of Shares	# of Likes	# of Comments	Reach	# of Clicks	# of Clicks to Website

EMAIL SUBSCRIBERS FROM FACEBOOK	
ENGAGEMENT	
Post with most shares	
Post with most likes	
Post with most comments	
Post with most clicks	

BOOSTS

Spend $	# of Shares	# of Likes	# of Comments	Reach	# of Clicks

FACEBOOK ADS

Spend $		Results	

Facebook Status Updates	Date	Time	✓

Campaign Manager

facebook MARKETING

Product / Service Campaign

Campaign	
Description	
Product / Service Newsletter Contest / Giveaway	
Start	End
Objective	
Target Audience	
Budget$ / Cost$ / Return$	
Landing Page	
Tracking Link	
Days and Time	
Winner / Date Notified	

Image

- ☐ Blog Post Announcement
- ☐ Blog Post Follow-up
- ☐ Autoresponder Setup
- ☐ Ad Campaign
  - Budget$
  - Cost$
  - Return$
  - Click Thru Rate
  - CPC (Cost per Click)
- ☐ Conversion Rate
- ☐ Hashtag
- ☐ Coupon Code (if applicable)

Advertising Campaign

Campaign	
Boost / Ad	
Description	
Start	End
Objective	
Target Audience	
Budget$ / Cost Per Day$	
Landing Page	
Tracking Link	

Text	Demographic

Image

Ad Planner

facebook
MARKETING

Campaign ______________________________

Title / Headline (25 Characters) ______________________________

Description (90 Characters) ______________________________

Detailed Text (200 Characters only seen on desktop) ______________________________

Call to Action ______________________________

Start & End Date ______________________________

Objective ______________________________

Target Audience ______________________________

Button ______________________________

Budget$ / Cost$ / Return$ ______________________________

Landing Page ______________________________

Tracking Link ______________________________

Reach ______________________________

Leads Generated ______________________________

Cost Per Lead ______________________________

Image

- ☐ Image
- ☐ Ad Copy
- ☐ Ad Distribution (Desktop or Newsfeed)
- ☐ Audience (Demographics + Interests)
- ☐ Ad Campaign
  - Budget$
  - Cost$
  - Return$
  - Click Thru Rate
  - CPC (Cost per Click)
- ☐ Conversion Rate

To Do

	Priority	Completed

Month

SUNDAY	MONDAY	TUESDAY	WEDNESDAY	THURSDAY	FRIDAY	SATURDAY

Notes

Acknowledge and Celebrate Your Success

Month:

Total Likes

Post with most engagement (shares, likes, comments) on Facebook

---

Post with most clicks

Blog post with most traffic from Facebook

This month I learned

A record I broke this month

My celebration this month

Next month I plan to do the same

Next month I plan to try (new)

Monthly Stats

GOAL:

Total Fans	New Fans	# of Posts	# of Shares	# of Likes	# of Comments	Reach	# of Clicks	# of Clicks to Website

EMAIL SUBSCRIBERS FROM FACEBOOK	
ENGAGEMENT	
Post with most shares	
Post with most likes	
Post with most comments	
Post with most clicks	

BOOSTS

Spend $	# of Shares	# of Likes	# of Comments	Reach	# of Clicks

FACEBOOK ADS

Spend $		Results	

Facebook Status Updates	Date	Time	✓

Campaign Manager

facebook MARKETING

Product / Service Campaign

Campaign	
Description	
Product / Service Newsletter Contest / Giveaway	
Start	End
Objective	
Target Audience	
Budget$ / Cost$ / Return$	
Landing Page	
Tracking Link	
Days and Time	
Winner / Date Notified	

Image

- ☐ Blog Post Announcement
- ☐ Blog Post Follow-up
- ☐ Autoresponder Setup
- ☐ Ad Campaign
  - Budget$
  - Cost$
  - Return$
  - Click Thru Rate
  - CPC (Cost per Click)
- ☐ Conversion Rate
- ☐ Hashtag
- ☐ Coupon Code (if applicable)

Advertising Campaign

Campaign	
Boost / Ad	
Description	
Start	End
Objective	
Target Audience	
Budget$ / Cost Per Day$	
Landing Page	
Tracking Link	

Text

Demographic

Image

Ad Planner

facebook MARKETING

Campaign ______________________

Title / Headline (25 Characters) ______________________

Description (90 Characters) ______________________

Detailed Text (200 Characters only seen on desktop) ______________________

Call to Action ______________________

Start & End Date ______________________

Objective ______________________

Target Audience ______________________

Button ______________________

Budget$ / Cost$ / Return$ ______________________

Landing Page ______________________

Tracking Link ______________________

Reach ______________________

Leads Generated ______________________

Cost Per Lead ______________________

Ad Planner

Image

- ☐ Image
- ☐ Ad Copy
- ☐ Ad Distribution (Desktop or Newsfeed)
- ☐ Audience (Demographics + Interests)
- ☐ Ad Campaign
  - Budget$
  - Cost$
  - Return$
  - Click Thru Rate
  - CPC (Cost per Click)
- ☐ Conversion Rate

To Do

	Priority	Completed

Notes

Editorial Calendar

facebook MARKETING

Month

SUNDAY	MONDAY	TUESDAY	WEDNESDAY	THURSDAY	FRIDAY	SATURDAY

Notes

Success Tracker

facebook MARKETING

Acknowledge and Celebrate Your Success

Month:

Total Likes

Post with most engagement (shares, likes, comments) on Facebook

---

Post with most clicks

Blog post with most traffic from Facebook

This month I learned

A record I broke this month

My celebration this month

Next month I plan to do the same

Next month I plan to try (new)

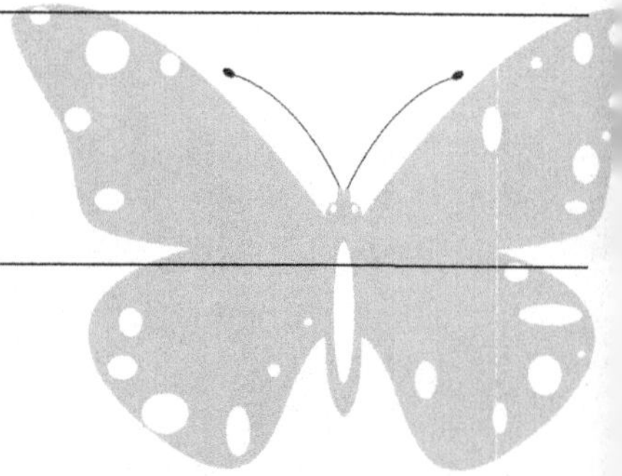

Monthly Stats

GOAL:

Total Fans	New Fans	# of Posts	# of Shares	# of Likes	# of Comments	Reach	# of Clicks	# of Clicks to Website

EMAIL SUBSCRIBERS FROM FACEBOOK	
ENGAGEMENT	
Post with most shares	
Post with most likes	
Post with most comments	
Post with most clicks	

BOOSTS

Spend $	# of Shares	# of Likes	# of Comments	Reach	# of Clicks

FACEBOOK ADS

Spend $		Results	

Status Updates

Facebook Status Updates	Date	Time	✓

Campaign Manager

facebook MARKETING

Product / Service Campaign

Campaign	
Description	
Product / Service Newsletter Contest / Giveaway	
Start	End
Objective	
Target Audience	
Budget$ / Cost$ / Return$	
Landing Page	
Tracking Link	
Days and Time	
Winner / Date Notified	

Image

- ☐ Blog Post Announcement
- ☐ Blog Post Follow-up
- ☐ Autoresponder Setup
- ☐ Ad Campaign
  - ○ Budget$
  - ○ Cost$
  - ○ Return$
  - ○ Click Thru Rate
  - ○ CPC (Cost per Click)
- ☐ Conversion Rate
- ☐ Hashtag
- ☐ Coupon Code (if applicable)

Advertising Campaign

Campaign	
Boost / Ad	
Description	
Start	End
Objective	
Target Audience	
Budget$ / Cost Per Day$	
Landing Page	
Tracking Link	

Text	Demographic
	Image

Ad Planner

facebook MARKETING

Campaign ______________________

Title / Headline (25 Characters) ______________________

Description (90 Characters) ______________________

Detailed Text (200 Characters only seen on desktop) ______________________

Call to Action ______________________

Start & End Date ______________________

Objective ______________________

Target Audience ______________________

Button ______________________

Budget$ / Cost$ / Return$ ______________________

Landing Page ______________________

Tracking Link ______________________

Reach ______________________

Leads Generated ______________________

Cost Per Lead ______________________

Ad Planner

facebook MARKETING

Image

- ☐ Image
- ☐ Ad Copy
- ☐ Ad Distribution (Desktop or Newsfeed)
- ☐ Audience (Demographics + Interests)
- ☐ Ad Campaign
  - Budget$
  - Cost$
  - Return$
  - Click Thru Rate
  - CPC (Cost per Click)
- ☐ Conversion Rate

To Do

facebook
MARKETING

	Priority	Completed

Editorial Calendar

facebook MARKETING

Month

SUNDAY	MONDAY	TUESDAY	WEDNESDAY	THURSDAY	FRIDAY	SATURDAY

Notes

Acknowledge and Celebrate Your Success

Month:

Total Likes

Post with most engagement (shares, likes, comments) on Facebook

---

Post with most clicks

Blog post with most traffic from Facebook

This month I learned

A record I broke this month

My celebration this month

Next month I plan to do the same

Next month I plan to try (new)

Monthly Stats

GOAL:

Total Fans	New Fans	# of Posts	# of Shares	# of Likes	# of Comments	Reach	# of Clicks	# of Clicks to Website

EMAIL SUBSCRIBERS FROM FACEBOOK	

ENGAGEMENT

Post with most shares	
Post with most likes	
Post with most comments	
Post with most clicks	

BOOSTS

Spend $	# of Shares	# of Likes	# of Comments	Reach	# of Clicks

FACEBOOK ADS

Spend $		Results	

Status Updates

Facebook Status Updates	Date	Time	✓

Campaign Manager

facebook
MARKETING

Product / Service Campaign

Campaign	
Description	
Product / Service Newsletter Contest / Giveaway	
Start	End
Objective	
Target Audience	
Budget$ / Cost$ / Return$	
Landing Page	
Tracking Link	
Days and Time	
Winner / Date Notified	

Image

- ☐ Blog Post Announcement
- ☐ Blog Post Follow-up
- ☐ Autoresponder Setup
- ☐ Ad Campaign
  - Budget$
  - Cost$
  - Return$
  - Click Thru Rate
  - CPC (Cost per Click)
- ☐ Conversion Rate
- ☐ Hashtag
- ☐ Coupon Code (if applicable)

Advertising Campaign

Campaign	
Boost / Ad	
Description	
Start	End
Objective	
Target Audience	
Budget$ / Cost Per Day$	
Landing Page	
Tracking Link	

Text	Demographic
	Image

Ad Planner

facebook MARKETING

Campaign ______________________

Title / Headline (25 Characters) ______________________

Description (90 Characters) ______________________

Detailed Text (200 Characters only seen on desktop) ______________________

Call to Action ______________________

Start & End Date ______________________

Objective ______________________

Target Audience ______________________

Button ______________________

Budget$ / Cost$ / Return$ ______________________

Landing Page ______________________

Tracking Link ______________________

Reach ______________________

Leads Generated ______________________

Cost Per Lead ______________________

Ad Planner

facebook MARKETING

Image

- [ ] Image
- [ ] Ad Copy
- [ ] Ad Distribution (Desktop or Newsfeed)
- [ ] Audience (Demographics + Interests)
- [ ] Ad Campaign
  - Budget$
  - Cost$
  - Return$
  - Click Thru Rate
  - CPC (Cost per Click)
- [ ] Conversion Rate

	Priority	Completed

Editorial Calendar

facebook MARKETING

Month

SUNDAY	MONDAY	TUESDAY	WEDNESDAY	THURSDAY	FRIDAY	SATURDAY

Notes

Acknowledge and Celebrate Your Success

Month:

Total Likes

Post with most engagement (shares, likes, comments) on Facebook

---

Post with most clicks

Blog post with most traffic from Facebook

This month I learned

A record I broke this month

My celebration this month

Next month I plan to do the same

Next month I plan to try (new)

Monthly Stats

GOAL:

Total Fans	New Fans	# of Posts	# of Shares	# of Likes	# of Comments	Reach	# of Clicks	# of Clicks to Website

EMAIL SUBSCRIBERS FROM FACEBOOK	

ENGAGEMENT

Post with most shares	
Post with most likes	
Post with most comments	
Post with most clicks	

BOOSTS

Spend $	# of Shares	# of Likes	# of Comments	Reach	# of Clicks

FACEBOOK ADS

Spend $		Results	

Status Updates

Facebook Status Updates	Date	Time	✓

Campaign Manager

facebook
MARKETING

Product / Service Campaign

Campaign	
Description	
Product / Service Newsletter Contest / Giveaway	
Start	End
Objective	
Target Audience	
Budget$ / Cost$ / Return$	
Landing Page	
Tracking Link	
Days and Time	
Winner / Date Notified	

Image

- ☐ Blog Post Announcement
- ☐ Blog Post Follow-up
- ☐ Autoresponder Setup
- ☐ Ad Campaign
  - Budget$
  - Cost$
  - Return$
  - Click Thru Rate
  - CPC (Cost per Click)
- ☐ Conversion Rate
- ☐ Hashtag
- ☐ Coupon Code (if applicable)

Advertising Campaign

Campaign	
Boost / Ad	
Description	
Start	End
Objective	
Target Audience	
Budget$ / Cost Per Day$	
Landing Page	
Tracking Link	

Text

Demographic

Image

Ad Planner

facebook MARKETING

Campaign ______________________________

Title / Headline (25 Characters) ______________________________

Description (90 Characters) ______________________________

Detailed Text (200 Characters only seen on desktop) ______________________________

Call to Action ______________________________

Start & End Date ______________________________

Objective ______________________________

Target Audience ______________________________

Button ______________________________

Budget$ / Cost$ / Return$ ______________________________

Landing Page ______________________________

Tracking Link ______________________________

Reach ______________________________

Leads Generated ______________________________

Cost Per Lead ______________________________

Ad Planner

facebook
MARKETING

Image

- ☐ Image
- ☐ Ad Copy
- ☐ Ad Distribution (Desktop or Newsfeed)
- ☐ Audience (Demographics + Interests)
- ☐ Ad Campaign
  - Budget$
  - Cost$
  - Return$
  - Click Thru Rate
  - CPC (Cost per Click)
- ☐ Conversion Rate

To Do

	Priority	Completed

Thank You

facebook MARKETING

HOPE YOU ENJOYED USING
YOUR FACEBOOK WORKBOOK AND PLANNER

GET YOUR FREE WEEKLY FACEBOOK PLANNER!
http://bit.ly/facebookweekly

PLEASE LEAVE A REVIEW ON AMAZON

BE SURE TO GRAB YOUR COPIES
- Social Media Marketing Workbook -
- Social Media Marketing Planner -
- Google+ Workbook and Planner -
- LinkedIn Workbook and Planner -
- Twitter Workbook and Planner -
- Pinterest Workbook and Planner -
- Instagram Workbook and Planner -

ALSO LOOK OUT FOR
Authentic Marketing – The Three E's of Online Marketing: Ethical, Effortless, Engaging
Social Media Marketing: How to Master Engagement in 15 Minutes a Day.

Connect with Dwainia Grey on LinkedIn, Google+, Facebook, Twitter, Pinterest and Instagram
dwainiagrey.me

Printed in Dunstable, United Kingdom

91222516R00092